Live and Love Life

Poems of Healing

Latrice Tillman

iUniverse, Inc.
Bloomington

Live and Love Life
Poems of Healing

iUniverse books may be ordered through booksellers or by contacting:

iUniverse
1663 Liberty Drive
Bloomington, IN 47403
www.iuniverse.com
1-800-Authors (1-800-288-4677)

ISBN: 978-1-4697-3812-3 (sc)
ISBN: 978-1-4697-3811-6 (hc)
ISBN: 978-1-4697-3813-0 (ebk)

Library of Congress Control Number: 2012900238

Printed in the United States of America

iUniverse rev. date: 02/15/ 2012

Dedication

This book is dedicated to my sister, Shuron Michelle Scott, who I miss dearly, and also to my son, K.J., who helped to initiate a true point of healing in my life.

Contents

Introduction

Have you ever felt alone and in need of encouragement but you wanted to resolve these feelings without actually having to talk to someone? This book contains a compilation of poems that were written during various times of need. Although created while feeling extremely weak, strengths were created from those weaknesses and now this book is being created to share these moments, in hopes of encouraging and motivating others to also overcome desperate times of need. When there is a need for encouragement and motivation, this book serves as a powerful resource. It can help anyone that is willing to accept help from someone else. Live and Love Life gives the opportunity for the audience to become encouraged, while also being entertained. Readers will enter a new realm of happiness and also have a greater strength and more motivation than they did prior to reading this literary work.

Acceptance

Bigger and Better

I am small.
Yes, you are bigger.
But, bigger is not better.
Hello bigger; I'm better.
Better is more than bigger.

Complete

Complete and whole—I am ...
Not made to feel complete, only if I have a man.
Yes, God has created a man that is perfect for me.
But, he's an addition to the woman I already exist to be.

Sometimes, desolate but lonesome is something that I never am.
Distance from all is a reserve and essential to God's plan.
Strength is developed out of weakness; especially during the
absence of man.
I can't always be present for all and neglect myself, only to drain
me of all that I am.

But, even in distance and being apart, together—we stand.
Solitude helps to refresh and thus far rejuvenates being human.
Sporadic distance from everyone and everything can be wholesome
and positive.
Consistent company and companionship are additions but not
required to live.

People, places, and things are only additions and catalysts, as I am
already existing.
I am primitive and fundamental, so there is nothing missing.
I'm the majority and God is my all and the primary. We are the
perfect equation.
All kinship after that are merely secondary relations.

Latrice Tillman

I have no need to put others down to help me to step up.
Being negative or decreasing in others does not give favorable
luck.
And no one on this earth has to speak or hold me still.
I am made whole and healed by a power that is ecstatically real.

No longer broken. Now, I'm resilient; therefore, allergic to
defeat.
Made perfectly as I am, I am whole and complete.

Hey world, this is me

Acceptance, approval, willing to accept.
Acceptance of who I am—God didn't make a mistake: He made me correct.
Thick hair. Nice when long. Cut it short and it quickly grows back.
I am the final, perfect copy of me. He didn't even need to make a draft.

My small, short frame with beautiful brown eyes.
Although never 20/20, enough to thank Him as I look up at the sky.
Doctor said, "she will be blind" and yet I came out with at least some vision.
Sensitiveness to illness but glad that I am living.

Used to have seizures but now check out the brain and mind.
People calling me genius, wise beyond my years and one of a kind.
Beautiful white teeth and I've learned to accept their size.
After all, they must be perfect, as people always compliment my beautiful smile.

Small ears but I can hear; better small than big.
But even if big, who cares—if to sound, they are receptive.
No huge breasts, no big butt, no big thighs, no big legs, no big hips.
Nose small and big simultaneously and the same with the lips.

Latrice Tillman

Sounds crazy I know but I refuse to take medicine, surgery, reduce, enlarge, or try to gain;

Then age more and have to undo and return to the doctor to fix again and again.

Body—attractive, as is my mind and spirit, which are most important and above all.

I love and accept myself and I stand with confidence—5 ft 3 inches physically—but mentally, I am very tall!

Hidden Treasure

Searching and searching but yet never to find,
As if only to discover and obtain in the mind.
Traveling and traveling—the distance is extremely expansive and
    so exceedingly far.
But to search far, not knowing it's near, is more than bizarre.
And yet so easily or just seemingly causing a loss to some . . .
Unfortunate only to discover when it's too late and long gone.
But not to worry because if it occurs once—can't it occur twice
    and many more?
Realization is vital to conquer and discover exactly what is being
    reached and striven for.
Whatever the desire—when exposed—stretch and reach, until it
    is touched.
But then upon conquer—is a realization that—already in
    existence—was such.

Judged and Stereotyped

Too small, too colorful, not enough. Too big, too dull, too much.
Too black, too white, lacking color. The wrong texture, not enough
   luster.
Too short, too soft, too tough. Too hot, too cold, too rough.

Too tall, too light, too dark. Not enough knowledge and experience,
   too smart.
Too wise, too open, too closed. Too many yes's, too many no's.
Too little faith, too many rich, too many poor. Too many choices,
   too many closed doors.

Too mean, too nice, too confused. Too much winning, too much
   to lose.
Too old, too young, too unforgiving. Too much of too—this and
   that—for living.
Hard to live, impossible to see with no eyes. Judgmental vision
   creates blindness and causes a substantial lively vision to die.

Self-discovery

When you settle for the sideline, you miss the champion in the
   game,
All because you allow yourself to be easily intimidated, but only
   you are to blame.
Why settle for losing—instead of taking a chance to win?
When given a 2nd chance, play hard from start to end.
Play exceedingly hard, like never ever before.
Thank God for 2nd chances and closing dead end doors.

Now, I recognize how silly of me to settle for so long,
Thinking I'm valueless and not worth much, so I would just keep
   accepting what was always wrong.
Of course, I didn't know any better but now I am set free.
Now I know who I am; yes, I have value and will never again
   accept what is beneath me.
What an affective lesson: it taught the great significance of a
   woman's worth.
If you don't know what and who you are, your life is truly lived
   like it is cursed.

So much misfortune and wondering why limitations and can only
   get so far ahead.
Then, when you shake free, you realize you were living as if
   dead.
Dead and empty inside, you were, and never could reach true
   happiness and peace.
Keeping company with those whose purpose was to keep you in
   defeat.

Latrice Tillman

Before returning to the dead phase, I'd rather be dead indeed.
But stepping back is never an option, as God always has better
for me.

It is vital to heal from life's pains or you'll seek fulfillment from
the wrong person when there's nothing they can give.
Eventually only added pains—unnecessarily—and more reasons
to die than live.
Young, lost, desperate, hurt, confused—was just trying to find my
way.
No more time and energy of such a huge mistake!
I finally healed the holes and tied the gaps: no more dead
weight.
I am glad to announce—I am here! I have finally arrived today!

Sister

Ever since she went away, my life hasn't been the same.
And knowing God needed her more does not take away the
  pain.
I miss her so much—she was my sister but also my best friend.
Her life ended and for me, a new painful life started to begin.

We would laugh, talk, and sing for hours, as if we were the same
  age.
She was 5 years older but she taught me so much; we were always
  on the same page.
As long as she was around, we could always find a reason to
  laugh.
Despite our lives not being perfect and her having to grow up
  fast.

Such warmth and protection—she was a mother by nature, even
  prior to my nephew,
And now she would be a grandmother because nephew has a
  few.
Funny to picture her as a granny—now it has been so much
  time . . .
Since I last saw or even dreamed about, but you still stay on my
  mind.

I know I'm in my 30s but I still yearn to once again have a big
  sister.
It hurt so badly when time came and ages matched up: All I
  could meditate on is how I missed her.

Latrice Tillman

Attempted to come and join you but now I know to wait until
it's my time.
Why is the pain just as fresh as yesterday and constantly in my
mind?

I wish I knew more to say on that day.
We said we loved each other and I watched you walk away.
I continued to stare until you were out of sight and I felt something
was wrong.
I just couldn't figure the feeling was telling me that you wouldn't
return home.
Although I said I love you, it wasn't enough: I have so much more
to say;
But, me and you haven't ended: I love you big sis and see you on
that day!

Window Shopping

Looking down, although she had plenty, she felt like it was never
  enough.
Thinking, "a new pair of shoes, because these seem to have a small
  scuff".
Fresh, crisp air on such a warm, lovely spring day—good for
  shopping so she trotted along her way;
With excess to spend and no limit to what she was willing to
  pay.

First stop—store so enticing with so many beautiful but eccentric
  shoes.
2 pairs didn't fit comfortably but yet she purchased and on—she
  moved.
2 pairs, 3 pairs, 4 pairs and sometimes she would only window
  shop . . .
Adoring what was on the other side but just for the brief
  moment—she stopped.

When she saw shoes so beautifully worn and tried by other
  customers inside . . .
Only then was when she was sure to venture in and give the shoes
  a try.
From the outside, looking in—the shoes appeared beautifully
  worn.
Humorously enough, she arrived home to try a pair again and
  how easily the shoe was torn.

Latrice Tillman

Expensively paid for; eccentric and embellished with designs and
   décor.
Such a huge price paid for shoes unfortunately not properly fitting
   because for others—the shoes are only customized for.

Within, Without

If you say oppose but they say agree,
Stand your ground and let them know what you mean.
Life is not about acceptance beyond the acceptance of one's self.
It's about loving yourself even when there is nobody else . . .
Around or loving you but you must continue to do well without
 and within.

Sometimes it's better to do without because when you lose, you
 learn to win.
When winning, there are places many and much can not go.
As you develop and travel your path, only carry along what helps
 you to grow.
When strong and hopeful within, the energy in transforms out
 and begins to manifest.
Don't conform to the norm; just be you because that's what you
 can be—the best.

Endurance

Eternal Dismay

A blue sky embodied by white clouds shaped like wings; but the
    wings' outline is filled with gray.
Numerous closed eyes and deaf ears but the lips are immutable as
    they part with much to say.
Emotionless and heartless, but the words attempt to express the
    feelings of someone else's blues.
Words with no meaning, feeling worse than a broken bone;
    bringing shame like when champions lose.

Bouncing off the enclosed walls of a dead end is lies, betrayal,
    hatred . . . so hard to forgive.
Causing more problems than disabling stress, but somehow I
    live.
Concealed secrets inside, how do I let it out?
It helps to talk about things; but, in this case . . . I doubt it.

My entire life has been a secret, will it all ever be told?
Put my story in a book . . . may be the bestseller ever sold.
How can I put it all behind—who can I blame?
It is not I, someone else deserves the fame.

It strikes harder than labor pain and it moves fast.
It's upsetting like ongoing dental pain . . . how long will it last?
How much longer can I run, fight, and pretend?
What I feel is slowly killing me within.

The burn is deeper than a chemical or fire could ever burn.
Spreads faster than disease, worse than the feeling of mourn.
Tears you faster than a machete, is hotter than a flame.
Please help me to stop it: I know God will take away the pain.

Latrice Tillman

Giving birth

Giving birth can be draining and full of extreme and torturous pain.

Amazing how that excruciating pain can produce such beauty.

Giving so much of yourself but simultaneously you also gain.

And after the birth has taken place, you have some new exciting duties.

The pain of birth is unfortunate but for what it brings forth . . .

Fruitful changes and strength come from pain and sorrow.

But, the sorrows and pains are affordable for their ultimate splendid worth.

What is pain and weakness today will produce pleasure and strength for tomorrow.

But, so much labor is involved before creation of a new life to live.

All that we go through is to propel us toward an embellished destiny;

A baby gives new gracious meaning to life and a grateful perspective;

Just as Goliath existed to promote David, some are promoted by the birth of a baby.

If you are going to give birth and your baby is a carnal baby, purpose or vision,

The only way to it is through it and inevitable pain is vital to the mission.

Giving Birth II

Although it may hurt, you must push, push, and push again.
Continue pushing throughout all of the pain.
For what waits, is a pleasure and a blessing indeed.
Pleasure produced after so much suffering and pain—hard to
  believe.
But, push, push, and push again.

Giving birth exemplifies an unexplainable gift.
It can shine the light on elements that may have otherwise been
  missed ...
Gives a new pair of eyes for a new sight to see.
More motivation than ever and another reason to exist and be.
So, push, push, and push again.

Push into empowerment; although, deliverance was through hurt
  and grief,
It's the channel most dreams travel and are birthed into reality—but
  only after so much perseverance, persistence, and belief.

My Way Out

My world is full of hell and everything just seems to fail.
I'm so stressed out—will I even live to tell . . .
Of good things not going right; bad things getting worse.
I'm living a miserable life—somebody tell what's wrong and
 explain the hurt.
How long will I be defeated; my mind is not always wrapped too
 tight.
It's not easy to do good and always stay open to the light.
Lord knows I try to do the right thing.
But, every now and then I have to loosen and let my heart sing.
Anger building up, tearing down this mind of mine.
I have to straighten up because time is flying.

Everything is falling down—being confused in my own world.
Too many pressures: I'm like a lost little girl.
But, in my own ways, I'm grown: There isn't a thing I can't see.
As I stress, my eyes are seeing things that people want to hide
 from me.
So, I sometimes escape this world riding on a cloud—high.
I don't do it for no reason and just to pass the time by.
But, when I slip out and under to another place,
Only some people will know by the blankness written on my
 face.
Sometimes, when my confidence gets too low,
I escape and find the perfect place to go.

I go there and get away from all of my depression.
And at that moment, this place gives me my progression.
I may not always be living life abundantly and might experience an occasional lack,
But, that can't get me down—knowing the clouds is where it's at.
Where what is at—you question and ask.
A place of peace where God helps me find a way and removes my mask.
It feels good to get it out and release thoughts off of my chest.
The more I write down, the more the stress is less.
No one ever told me life could or would be alright.
So, I had to find out for myself and utilize something that I actually like.
This is my way to escape all messed up, none-sense issues.
With God as my light, I have a better visual.

Never Give Up!

When the tree branches, limbs, and stumps give way to the wind;

When no one is around and it seems you have not one friend;

When the load is heavy and there isn't much more you can bare;

When everything is failing but no one seems to care;

When the pavement has run out and the road has come to an end;

When you can see a finish line and no new place to begin;

When the load you carry is so heavy and you can't help but fall;

When nothing you've done is working even though you have given it your all;

When all backs are turned to you and your back is against the wall;

When you've fallen so low, you can barely even crawl;

When all doors are shut and you have ran out of luck,

Just know God loves you and yet and still—you should never give up!

The Invisible Storm

The wind is blowing and the trees sway back and forth extremely
hard.

The rain is dropping, as if from big buckets of water being poured
by God.

The sky is dark and cloudy; The sun hasn't shone in days.

The road is unclear and the sign points in too many different
ways.

So much turmoil and debris floating around in the air.

Houses shaking, foundations cracking, trash and trees floating
and flying everywhere.

Lightning flashing, thunder roaring causing so much confusion.

Time is even running away and winning has given way to losing.

Unlimited disturbances and so many colors and particles of
dangerous haze.

The mind is trapped in a tornado of confusion and can't seem to
find it's way.

Deep in a hole of emptiness where nothing and no one else is
even there.

But, when the eyes become opened, this place is not truly there.

Actually, all is still: all that has been in movement is the mind.

But, God can calm the storm and only then will things be
controlled and redefined.

Latrice Tillman

Faith and Hope

Another Generation

Seconds lead to minutes to hours to days.
Weeks lead to months to years to decades.

Winter, Spring, Summer, Fall—seasons change.
All things change although change remains the same.

Weaknesses lead to failures and failures to success.
Weaknesses to the worst and the worst to the best.

Mental, spiritual, physical, emotional—domains transform.
Each persists, although it is to the physical that most conform.

Thoughts lead to feelings to beliefs to actions.
The actions then confirm the thoughts and leads to deeper
    passions.

A seed gets planted and blossoms in due time.
Adequate nurturing and attention contribute to a result that is
    divine.

Negative can always result in positive; all roads lead somewhere.
An important influential element is a measure of care.

As all things work together and help each other to bloom and
 grow,
The next generation must be fed, given hope, and taught which
 way to go.

Contribute to the next breed and family heritage: they need to
 be led.
Train them and they will grow according to how they were fed.

Latrice Tillman

Change for the better

There is oh so little, but yet oh so much . . .
Without and empty but the cup is filling up.
Pinching from nothing but yet something is revealed.
Numb and emotionless but yet so much he can feel.
Lonely and isolated but much company he keeps.
Atmosphere—motionless as much is released.
Running and running but going nowhere fast.
Will it always get worse and how long will it last?

Just as an unattractive caterpillar transforms into a beautiful
butterfly;
Or eagles learn to soar to a height where no other can fly and be
so high;
Or as muscles are painfully worked to produce enduring
strength,
Pain converts into pleasure and a new beginning follows an end.
Sometimes, what it takes is a storm and rainy, gloomy
weather . . .
To recognize luster and how the storm contributed to the
luminous vision, which caused change for the better.

Close the old, Open the new

Something is telling me yes, but something is telling me no.
Holding on to the past, when I need to be letting go.
Dwelling on pain from the past and glancing behind;
Instead of focusing straight ahead and moving forward with
time.

And so I must decide to open up and release the pain.
And upon release, I'm open and available to gain.
Either fear or have courage; both can not occur simultaneously.
Either look behind in the past or forward in the future; it is to be
or not to be.

A new opportunity—grab it tight or loose and let it go.
But why let go before completely getting it and then of course,
I'll never know …
Know the better, the positive because instead I chose the pit of
fear.
To continue falling deeper into a dark place and when I cry—no
one can hear.

Fear whispering "no" into my ear is not the least bit of a friend.
But the courage that is saying "yes" only hopes to help restore,
rejuvenate, and mend.
When courage knocks at the door or rings the phone, answer the
call.
Don't invite pain and fear in because they are only trying to trip
me up and make me fall.

Latrice Tillman

Life

Life is precious and even a child understands it is a joy; the
following was written by an 8 year old boy:

Love is something good that you want.
Inside is something that you want to protect but . . .
Faith is what you should believe and
Enjoy life because life is good.

My son is a writer also as you can see; The first letter to each
above line is L I F E!

Splitting Agony

Sharp as the rigid edge of a brand new scalpel as it divides layers
of skin;
Stretched far wide and beyond—like the ocean—don't know
beginning from end.
Feels like surgical incisions with no anesthesia and yet wide
awake,
Or the roof and walls caving in and crushing every bone like in
the occurrence of an earthquake.
It crushes bone by bone as you encounter boulders while falling
and tumbling downhill.
Having the worst nightmare then wake up only to determine it
is real.
Intense and piercing like a labor spasm that refuses to end.
It refuses to give up and strikes again and again.
Flesh splits and separates from left to right and right to left.
What a great rip it leaves as it tries to push one to death.
Screaming and crying that you've had enough and can take no
more,
Confused at how you've lasted this long and don't know what
you're living for,
Tired of these episodes and a lack of solid purpose, direction, and
aim.
It hurts so badly, only God takes away such pain!

Latrice Tillman

Who am I

I run to the left but end up on the right.
I run up but end up going down.
I run to safety but end up facing a plight.
I smile hard but end up with a frown.

I try to protect but instead I destroy.
I plan for success but instead I fail.
I plot honest tactics but end up with a ploy.
I practice healthy living but get further from being well.

I turn on the light but yet I'm still in the dark.
I try my best to do right but end up doing wrong.
I try to put out the fire but instead I start a new spark.
I try to shorten the unnecessary path but instead make it even
    more long.

I try to start a good work but instead cause one to end.
I try to end foolery but instead cause more to begin.
I try to go straight but instead I bend.
I bring destruction and damage when all I wanted to do was
    mend.

I give my all just to try to encourage and motivate;
Hoping to bring out the best but instead of love—I produce
    hate.
This is what the enemy reveals but—push! Do not agree!
How could this be true if the same God that resides above in
    Heaven also abides in you and me?!

Focus

Deprivation

Luxurious houses to live in; fancy cars to drive.
Capable of traveling by any means, including a private jet to fly.
Traveling far and beyond seeing the beauty of many lands.
Needs abundantly supplied; provided with more than he can fully
stand.
Diamonds and jewels; unending wealth; assets and values; nothing
but the best.
But on the other side is a man who has much less.

No dwelling to call home and lacks resources to evade or take a
pleasurable drive.
Needs not met and no one to help lessen pain or provide.
Extremely lost; needing and searching for direction, purpose, a
sign, a guide ...
Without an abundance of a rich lifestyle, his misery is hard to
hide.
Lingering out in the cold, only wishing for warmth and perhaps
even a friend.
Intense distressing weather and circumstances along with broken
pieces that can't reform or mend.
Stuck in a warp zone: time dissipates and appears lost.
But, in actuality, he possesses all, by means of expensive costs.

It is only his inner life and spirit that lacks peace and happiness
although he is absolutely financially set.
His intrinsic values are so robustly disheartening, as he doesn't
realize the true wealth.

The tangible is becoming intangible because it is something that can't touch his heart.
Although he possesses all in the physical, there are more elements required to keep him from falling apart.
Love, life, health, family, and so many, many more . . .
Makes life worth living and are the true gifts by which life—we can genuinely and indefinitely adore.

Latrice Tillman

Focused

It's 2012 and playtime is over and out.
People don't seem to know what life is truly all about.
. . . so focused on others instead of getting right for self.
I follow and focus on God and not everybody else.
I protect me because (beside God) no one else will.
I don't do evil for evil but if that's how they think, then that's just
how they feel.
People trying to judge and question my way.
He who is without sin—cast the first stone, is what the Bible
say.

I don't exist to prove myself or worry about what people say;
Cause they're always going to talk, but unfortunately the talking
wont make me fade.
If they stay cursed when I stay blessed and I'm relaxing while they
are stressed,
They should be more like me and run with the best.
Forget people—only God is the best.
Give your mind, heart, & worries to Him & He'll handle the
rest.
Everybody's mind is on me but I'm focusing hard…
I see nothing and nobody but God!!

Motivation

Motivation can help to keep focus and purpose in perspective.

Ever since he came along, I've begun to reject being rejected.

He helped me to get my focus aligned just right.

Ever since he came along, my vision hasn't been blurry; I've had a clear sight.

I finally felt love and I learned to give it.

I inhaled happiness and so I learned to live it.

He gave me a boost of energy and strength to persevere and endure so much more.

My mind became open and I learned to deeply explore.

I was sleepwalking but since his arrival, I became awake.

I would have never guessed the impact that such a presence could make.

Latrice Tillman

And now I protect his existence with all of my being.

His presence has given my life a new beautiful meaning.

I've became the best person that I didn't think I could be.

Because of my son, I am the best version of me.

Gratitude

Amazing

Amazing how the rain and clouds can go away and the sun suddenly appear.
Amazing how the dangerously slippery wet roads dry, as away—goes the atmosphere of the drear.
Amazing how the one desperately calling for help was finally heard and rescued.

Amazing how the last one finally was first and found his way.
Amazing how yesterday they gave up but yet are still here today.
Amazing how they were once abandoned but are no longer destitute.

Amazing how situations do not forever remain negative, unfortunate, and bad.
Amazing how negative converts into positive and zero converts to inconceivable abundance that one never had.
Amazing how something so finished, done, and old is replenished and made new.

Dedication

I don't know how to say this, so I will just jump right in,
And start but there's so much I want to say, and don't know where
    to begin.
This is a dedication to my true support team,
As I realize that having your unconditional love, for so many
    years, is truly a dream.

You are 100 with me: you don't Jekyll and Hyde behind my
    back,
Or try to know everything, as long as you have the relevant
    facts;
And if I call right now at 3 a.m., I know you will be there,
To show me true love and concern because you genuinely care.

What I don't understand is how you are moved because you feel
    when I'm in pain,
And you never try to put me down or take my spot just so you
    can gain.
Never a competition or overlooking who I am and that there's
    nothing I can't do,
Because you truly see and treat me like I'm a queen and I'm
    grateful for you.

Always supporting and encouraging me and never trying to use
    me,
And you definitely don't stand back and agree to someone trying
    to abuse me.

But, how you see me as so much better than I can see myself,
Is beyond my comprehension, but yet I appreciate your kind
words and consistent help.

I guess all I'm trying to say is I have no doubts that what we have
is true;
And the same love that you have for me is the love I feel for you.
I thank God for placing you in my life and without you, I don't
know what I would do;
But, I thank you for showing me what's true & unconditional,
and for it, I love you.

Purpose

He came to her on a morning so blue and gray,
Like Santa Claus coming in the middle of a summer day.
Everyone is scared of him; even a lion has this feeling of fear,
Because he steals things so precious and dear.
She was only fifteen years when death stole her away.
But, God continues to carry me to this very day.
I miss my sister so much; she was my best friend.
However, I know we will be reunited. We will meet again.

The sorrows of life can be heavy and so confusing;
Which is why I stick with God—because He keeps me from
    losing.
Although I was confused and could not understand why;
If only I had been given a sign, I could have said goodbye.
No, I would not have said goodbye. I would've grabbed her
    hand,
And we would've crossed over together into the much better
    land.
But, now I understand it was necessary to help fulfill the purpose
    within me.
I am grateful for my life, as I am made strong through weaknesses
    and God continues to lead.

Latrice Tillman

What's one without the other?

It's not easy to recognize up until you go down.
But, could you recognize being high if there was no low?
Sometimes, you don't know you're lost until you've been found.
And because life moves so fast, can you appreciate when the time
   moves slow?

It's hard to appreciate sunshine until you go through the rain,
And you might not be able to recognize pleasure without the
   pain.

If day never came, would you learn to love the night?
And can you learn to appreciate good and dwell less on bad?
Without day, it would always be dark and you would wish for light.
But with appreciation, you can create more happy than sad.

What would happen without God's creation of woman for man?
Who would help woman to sit or man to stand?

What is the value of full at the time of empty?
What is the difference between sweet and sour, if something is
   bittersweet?
Could you recognize a friend if you had not one enemy?
The confusion is the same but either you have a win or you have
   a defeat.

One lacks value without the other but both are inevitable just like the inevitable joys of life before inevitable death.

Love

Burnout

What to do? Who to blame?
Tired, frustrated, energy drained.
So much to do, so little time.
Loss of control, losing the mind.
Go to work, go to school.
Exercise the body and also the mind too.
Spiritual studies and meditation.
Send the child to school and help with his education.
Volunteer in the community; help family and friends.
Cook, clean, leisure time with the child; the day never ends.
Forcing time for self, just to relax and maintain.
Daily duties maintained and most will never change.
After daily duties, barely any time for self care.
Not to mention the days with meetings or extra business affairs.
What kind of life is this? To give and give and never take.
To neglect the self is a huge mistake.
Needing time for refreshment, restoration, and nurturing for the self.
Help is good but no good if self is neglected and last after all else.

Caring

When the phone rings—always pick up and answer the call.
When they trip—rush in and be the cushion before they fall.
Give and medicate them when they are hurt or sick.
Adjust the clothes and shoes, just to make them fit.
Run to the rescue and bandage the pain.
Create a fallacy of sun to take away their rain.
When the tank or account depletes down to empty,
Replace and fill up even though it's getting close to one's own
    last penny.

When the clock stops—squeeze in the 25th hour of the day;
Just to take on the responsibilities of others and help them make
    a way.
Climb a mountain and jump hurdles even with broken legs.
Trying to drive straight but going in circles instead.
Always there to answer the beckon call of others.
But now that the storm is over here, they have left and ran for
    cover.
Always running to them just to have them run the other way.
But, now it seems obvious that only one thing is not a facade;

You do all you can and for others, you're always there;
But, when it's concerning you, no one even cares.
It's good and great to help others but not to the extreme,
That you lack love and care for yourself and give up your own
    dream.

If people take so much from you and demand that you take from
  yourself,
Depart fast and far from them and take up company with
  somebody else.
People that use, abuse, and demand they be put above you,
Are unaware of your value—so depart to better company because
  somebody truly does love you!

Kidnapped

Kidnapped; she's trying to escape and get back.
But, she's so distraught and lost and doesn't know where she's at.

He has her tied down so tightly; restricted; she can barely move.
So weak; can't see far ahead, so dizzy, so confused.

How did this happen? She never even saw him coming.
If only given a warning—she could have taken off running.

Nevertheless, he has captured her, and now it seems she is stuck.
Fighting so hard; but, no closer to escaping. So, she's giving up.

He has touched her spirit, stolen her mind, robbed her of her heart.
She wants to get them back, but he has already picked them apart.

No longer are they hers for he has completely conquered—the
  exact moment he grabbed.
They are in his possession and most of all—her heart—he has
  kidnapped.

Love Confession

Not a 4 page letter or another love song;
Just thoughts and feelings from a mental diary, a pen, and paper
to put them on.
So many years passed and still no one can compare.
Even with years devoured by someone that should have never
been there.

Mind spinning; tossing and turning; playing games in my own
mind.
Crazy—can't voice this confession—even after so much time.
Don't want to seem psycho, crazy, or obsessed.
Keeping silence reduces the anxiety no less.

Eventually just might go crazy from keeping it bottled in . . .
Or burst like pressure in pipes; either way, it has to come from
within.
Disbelief, state of paralysis, can't move, can't confess . . .
Tried so hard but so lethargic; can't even give an effort of my
best.

From one life phase to another, as it continues to be . . .
A standing emotion—residing in the head and heart and it refuses
to delete.
Impossible, unbelievable, ridiculous; this type of thing doesn't
happen or exist;
So, just bury the bone and never open the closet.

But I'm in love with me and what will denial solve?
Disguising, hiding truth is no good; find courage and get issues
    resolved.
Glad to discover love for self being greater than ever before.
This new discovery has presented a life that can't help but be
    adored.

One for all

What is love—he's trying to figure it out.
What is this thing that everyone keeps talking about?
How does it look? How does it feel?
Does it really exist? Is it really real?
How does it exist if he is here and she is there?
Surely, God has at least one for all on the shelf . . .
A customized gift and each can have his own.
Although seeming an endless, hopeless journey—to one his heart
    will belong.

It is only right and true when delivered by God.
An elite man, an elite woman—no need to put up an emotional
    guard.
Full commitment, communication, and trust.
A bond that can last even if not giving in to lust.
If not patiently awaited for, it can not be true.
While patiently waiting, God will send hope, strength, and also
    renew.
Sent to an already complete person as the mate won't complete
    the person—but a purpose.
A help and team mate to help support and keep the focus.
But, the gift will be sent when there are no built up walls.
Deliveries are scheduled. There is one customized for each; one
    for all.

Real love

Too often, I may not be serious or not serious enough.
But yet and still, He gives me everlasting love.
After so much time, I sometimes feel confused still.
Luckily for me, it doesn't change the way He feels.
Yes, I love Him and my love is real.
Anything He wants me to do—I will.

At times, my actions are wrong and instead, I should yield.
This is a love I refuse to ruin and want to continue to build.
Actions speak louder than words and this is too deep to just tell.
But, He knows my heart and He knows me particularly well.
My actions do speak louder but sometimes when I speak—I
    choke.
I do want Him to know I can never let Him go.

And if I tried or even thought about it, my heart would say no.
He is my entire life and I try my best to show Him so.
I float on a cloud when I hear his voice.
And His presence is unexplainable and is way more than
    enough.
There are no words to express His love or touch.
But, those three words He says to me, means so much.

Even though he has this same relationship with others, we will
    never be through.
Our relationship doesn't change just because God loves me just
    like He also loves you.

Latrice Tillman

Spiritual Meeting

Minds have talked; spirits have touched.

How is it possible to communicate so much?

How is it possible to see without the eye and speak without the mouth?

Words of certainty are loudly spoken with no doubt.

Surely, what is spoken and seen is not a facade and to hear—without ears?

Can't be imagination as the sound is so loud, perceivable and clear.

And to feel—without a physical touch?

A meeting of spirits—even without physical senses—can reveal so very much.

Lips making words but the words say nothing as the speaking is silent.

Ears hearing but the sound is merely vibrant.

Nothing more than a vibration; eyes visualizing but there is nothing to see.

Feeling so much even when numbness is existentially.

Confused senses, a hurting mind from trying to figure what it could be.

And then a thought of revealing—just a supernatural encounter of when spirits meet.

Latrice Tillman

Tranquility

Rockin' and Rollin'; Hippin' and Hoppin'
Jumping and Skipping; Poppin' and Lockin'
Breakin', Old school, New school
Country, Classical and Blues
Opera, Rap, Hip Hop
Alternative, Contemporary, Classic Rock
Broadway, Soul, Jazz, R & B
Reggae, Latin, Symphony . . .
Makes me move, composes and motivates me.
What soothes and inspires you to move your feet?

Warning

Love, how do you know? How are you informed?
When it is coming, no one will forewarn.

More often unprepared than ready and willing.
Some claim it falsely because they haven't experienced the true
feeling.

But if love is not first for one's self,
It is impossible to make it readily available to someone else.

Pain, confusion, loneliness breeds desperation . . .
Desperation and togetherness among those unprepared eventually
goes from together to separation.

Love doesn't have nor does it build on an unstable ground.
It doesn't put you on a carousel of hurt and continuously take you
around and around.

It is not mean, love is inviting and kind;
Best enjoyed when shared by people of alike minds.

Love doesn't fear so the heart becomes open and adjusts . . .
Takes wrongs with rights; not a synonym for lust . . .

Is a natural part of living and loving life.
It gives more than takes and hope does abide.

Latrice Tillman

There is no competition and loved ones always remain side by
    side.
Jealousy does not exist and there is no such thing as pride.

It endures all things and stands strong.
If it does not possess such characteristics—it is questionable: to
    what—are you holding on.

Time

Killing Time

So much earth shattering noise but yet so calm and quiet.
A heavenly peace disturbed by the uproar of an emotive riot.
Utterly gloomy and dark but yet so much heavenly light.
Indeed blind, as there is complete absence of sight.
Movement slow and inert, but yet lightning fast.
What time does—when waiting for it to past.

Tired of waiting; anticipation can build no more.
But killing time in such a way only closes a door . . .
To peace and joy; when one should enjoy each second in time,
Instead of wishing it away and being a prisoner in the mind.
Forcing illness internally when the external is so well;
There's grand vitality in releasing negative and choosing not to
    dwell.

Things will come and occur whenever they may.
Why whisk away enjoyment—while one is to wait?
Realize—while quiet outside, noise was solely within.
Only opening eyes was required to bring the noise to an end.
Inner—worse than outer and all in the mind is utterly real . . .
Causing one to be dizzy, even when everything is still.

One can be free in the world—and yet—a prisoner in the mind.
But—it's no way to live: It only kills person and time.

Mind over Matter

Greatest gifts can come in the smallest package and arrive when
   unexpected.
Some gifts are better received after experiences of being rejected.
But yet, rushing to insignificance and trading out vitality,
Instead of maintaining the endurance for what is to be later
   received;
And trading now for later, being anxious and eager can certainly
   cost.
Debating with time is but a certain lost.

And where is the logic in a continuation of debate . . . .
If the ultimate is promised—just you wait.
Ordering rush delivery has a high cost but why pay more?
When either way—the gift will arrive at the front door.
It only seems the gift is accompanied by immeasurable time.
Truly, it is simply mind over matter—don't dignify matter over
   mind.

Release Time

Oh how I wish life could be perfect, but it's not a promise God
    has made.
Pain from the past can easily continue on into today.
Disgusted; fearful, hurtful, negative emotions and effects still
    remain.
Fighting in your head to catch amnesia and for some reason, you
    take the blame.
One occurrence too many—can only make it worse,
So then life is unquestionably starting to feel like a curse.
On top of being told what you aren't and what you can't do,
Best friend dies and no one is protecting you.

All is forgiven but years later—still remaining scars;
Uncontrollable anxiety and the constant wonder of who people
    actually are.
No one can be trusted: it's not worth letting them get close.
Seems to be a case of misfortune overdose,
With teary eyes, a knotted stomach, and skin beginning to
    crawl;
Because of a few, there is a lack of desire of closeness to all.
Experiences of life causes one to easily run or turn away,
And not establish intimacy as to maintain comfortable distance
    and space.

But past occurrences should not continue to control one's life.
Proverbs 20:3—walk away from strife.
One day, there will be complete openness and
    trust—wholeheartedly;

But, only as led by the Spirit and not allowing control from events of the past to proceed.

It is a choice and only an individual's choice to make indeed.

Personal strength is from the Lord, who has already set the person free.

He covers and protects now, so the past should be let loose and released.

If continuing to grasp the past, the beauty of life can not possibly conquer the beast.

Time

Before time ends and all in existence drops,

Before the ticking ceases and the clock stops,

Before infinity never arrives,

Before time gives in and agrees to die,

Before indefinitely ceases to pass ...

Never will occur and opportunities will cease, as distinction occurs
fast.

Today and also tomorrow will be yesterday.

Chances will be passed up and gone away.

If ever to do something, do it now my friend.

Time waits for no one; do it now, before time ends.

Tomorrow is Today

An infinite maze; where there is always a place to run and a place to hide.
Always another day so when tomorrow arrives and even today, stand boldly with pride;

But, life menacing events and unendurable pain have you scorned, hurt, torn, chastised, mistreated, beat down.
The brutal cuts and deep gashes will close and heal, so survive until tomorrow and smile instead of frown.

Bound by unjust imprisonment; told what not to do, what you can't do, and that all is impossible,
Faith is the key of release. Just know that you can be a leader of tomorrow that others can follow;
Instead of living in the land of being unintelligent, unattractive, incapable, deformed,
And also unworthy in addition to everything else that has been forcibly learned.

Lies! Lies! Lies! This land is a hallucination and tomorrow it will be seen . . .
That it's a fantasy created by others and all lies and lacks true and vital meaning.

Hard to accept self worth because what is perceived.
But, the real value starts with what is believed.

Latrice Tillman

Demolish the negative; explore the validity and value within,
And realize that to have a great ending, a great journey must
begin.
Discard misconceptions from the lies of the past and present
day,
As to lead to a better, beautifully envisioned way.

Wounds still unhealed, yielding to pain, still twisted, unable to
get straight?
Prolong the new journey no longer—tomorrow is today.